SOUTHWARK AT WAR

A book of memories and photographs
compiled and edited by Rib Davis and Pam Schweitzer

Local Studies Library
1996

Published 1996

ISBN 0 905849 19 1

A British Library Cataloguing in Publication
A catalogue record for this book is available from
the British Library.

CONTENTS

Cover photograph: A Heinkel over the docks in 1940. Courtesy of the Imperial War Museum.
Rear cover: Gas mask drill outside the Red Cross premises, 160 Peckham Rye, c 1939.
Courtesy of Mr & Mrs Charlesworth.
All other photographs are from Southwark Local Studies Library or the contributors.

SOUTHWARK AT WAR

This publication forms part of a reminiscence project to record and celebrate the lives of people in Southwark during the war years. Co-ordinated by Pam Schweitzer and Rib Davis of Age Exchange Theatre Trust and Reminiscence Centre for Southwark Libraries and Education Service

The project has involved many tape-recorded individual interviews, group interviews and discussions and the collecting of photos. These materials have then contributed to an exhibition held at the Elephant and Castle, a specially commissioned play *When the Lights Come on Again* which has played to young and old across the Borough, an education pack for use in schools and colleges, a permanent set of resources of tapes, photos and transcripts and, of course, this book.

The editors wish to thank the following for their contributions to the project:

Eleanor Ala
Kathleen Ash
Doris Bailey
Gladys Bailey
Flo Ball
Tom Ball
Gladys Beechey
Violet Bennett
Elsie Blenkey
Sabina Brookes
Esther Cadge
Irene Cambridge
Edith Cheshire
Elizabeth Cole
Doreen Davis
Edna Davis
Mary Davis
Mr Davis
Lydia Dawkins
Phylis Dean
Betty Dix
Ethel Dorney
Mr Elden
Mary Ellmore
Gladys Fish
Joe French
Bill Gibson
Mary Gibson
Tehiay Gough-Yates
Mrs Gregory
Jean Hawks
Arthur Holyhead
Milly Jackson
Miss Kearne
Ron Kendrick
Sam King
Miss Lane
Vera Law
Mr Leigh
Mrs Leigh
Doris Mahoney
Ivy Maylan
Mrs McBrian
Mary McNulty
Win Mitchell
Audrey Normington
Betty Notley
Anne O'Connor
Bill O'Sullivan
Bridie O'Sullivan
Eileen O'Sullivan
Lil Patrick
Joan Piper
Doris Platt
Deborah Playne
Doris Prickett
Jeanne Quick
Mrs Quinlan
Barbara Rawle
Norman Rawle
Miss Reeves
Ivy Richardson
May Roberts
Mr Samson
Joe Scala
Stella Scanlon
Louise Sedgewick
Joe Seeley
Grace Shelford
Grace Smith-Grogue
Flo Spike
Doris Stevenson
Rosina Strange
Whinnie Tilbury
Lilley Tindale
Mary Tlouter
Mr Todd
Mrs Todd
Mary Trivett
Queenie Turner
Hilda Ward
Gertrude Watkins
Rose Watts
Leonard Whitlock
Iris Wilkins
Bill Winter
Doreen Woods
Ellen Wright
Jessie Yabsney

Special thanks also to Janice Brooker, Stephen Humphrey, Stephen Potter and Len Reilly of Southwark Local Studies Library and also, Julian Heather and Dominic Bean and the rest of the staff of Southwark Library Service, Southwark Leisure and the Southwark Education Service.

INTRODUCTION

What is now the Borough of Southwark has altered almost out of recognition in the years of this century. The most profound changes took place as a result of the Second World War, transforming forever not only the landscape but also the ways of life of the people of the borough. If we are ever to come to terms with the present we must have some understanding of the past, so this book not only marks the 50th anniversary of the end of the war - recording and celebrating the experiences of those who lived here through those momentous years - but also puts into perspective the lives we lead now.

History is very often presented as a series of famous names and events, but in fact we all play our part in creating - and living through - history; this book tells the story of the war years in Southwark using the words of ordinary local people. It was these 'ordinary' people who endured the day-to-day experiences of being under attack, coping with shortages, being shunted around the country. It is their memories which are presented here, along with photographs which also portray the everyday life of the borough. Some of the tape-recorded interviews we held were of individuals, some of groups, in which the reminiscences of one would jog the memories - good and bad - of another. We hope their stories may also jog your memory a little.

Southwark at War records a huge range of experiences, from the ferocious bombing of the industrial and dockland areas of the north of the borough in the early years to the fierce rocket attacks on the south towards the end of the war. We learn of women holding the fort, taking on new responsibilities, looking after each other and finding new comradeship. We learn of the enormous amount of work conducted by Civil Defence organisations, of firewatching involving men and women who were also doing other work in the day. There was some fun to be had here during the war but also a huge amount of work.

Many Southwark children were, of course, evacuated during the war, some to idyllic rural life, rather more perhaps to places where they felt out of place or plain unwelcome. While the 'phoney war' continued many returned to Southwark, only then to find themselves at the heart of the Blitz. Once more large numbers left, returning again to London during the relative calm of the middle period of the war, yet this time soon finding themselves under rocket attack. All the traumas - and, in a few cases, the delights - of youth in wartime are reflected in their reminiscences.

Maintaining some sort of family life in this bombarded part of London was a hard business during the war. Menfolk were often abroad, children and perhaps older people in other parts of the country, women out to work. In addition there was the rationing and shortages to cope with. Yet the end of the war, the joyful but often painful reuniting of families and communities, also brought its own enormous problems in terms of both personal relationships and physical circumstances. Many young parents who had hardly seen each other for years had had their beliefs and assumptions radically altered by their wartime experiences. Now, crammed with their children into their in-laws' back room in Bermondsey or Peckham, they did not have an easy time of it.

It has been a privilege for us to meet these people and talk about their wartime experiences. We have been saddened, entertained, amazed and moved. We have also learned a great deal. We hope you gain as much from reading this book.

Rib Davis and Pam Schweitzer

A view looking north towards Tower Bridge across the Gainsford Street area of Bermondsey.

EVACUATION

We all thought there was going to be a full-scale war, panic stations. We all got ready to go away. When they announced it - they were evacuating us to Rye - I was on Denmark Hill station and all of us was there crying our eyes out. We'd all had to pack our bags for twelve o'clock. We were waiting to get on a train. In came the train and before we got on we heard the siren go. They thought they were going to come over right away and start bombing, so they bundled us all in the train and we didn't have time to say goodbye or anything. We were all pushed into the train and off we went. We didn't know where we were going. All the signs were all wiped out. You didn't know where you were. You couldn't say because if you opened your mouth you didn't know who was listening.

Mrs Bennett

We were in this church, sitting down there and some official person would come round and say, "This lady's going to take you." It was like an auction sale to me. "This person will take a mother and one child. This person has enough room for a mother and three children." Or, "This person will take you if you could do her housework."

Mrs Bennett

I had started to teach when war broke out. On the 1st September, I was teaching on the Old Kent Road: we were evacuated. There was lots and lots of children went. They came to school with their rucksacks on and things. From Waterloo station we were taken on a train to Yeovil in Somerset. When we got down there the reception was quite good. We were taken to the factory. They were making 'survival cheese'. They had milk, biscuits, ready for the children and everybody. Then we were taken to a big school to be sent out to different homes. That's where the arrangements in Yeovil went wrong. Some of our children were put in one of the worst streets in Yeovil that you can imagine, really poverty stricken. One of our staff was put in a house where the sheets were dirty on the bed. She said, "I can't stay there."

Elsie Blenkey

I was chosen and my brother was chosen at the same time, which left my sister. I said, "I'm not going to go until my sister's got somewhere to go." We were supposed to be kept together. But nobody wanted three children. Anyway, she was fortunate enough. She was selected by a lady, a spinster, her and her sister lived together. They came up about half an hour, three quarters of an hour after we had been selected, which made it a lot easier. At least I knew I could write back home and say, "We've all got a place to go." Got somewhere to write to - this is the thing. Because some of them were left. They weren't chosen for two, three, four days, some of them, and they had to sleep at school.

Bill Winter

The horrible thing about it was you were taken all away, all put in a school hall and they came round and picked you out. If you looked nice, you were picked out. But it you were some poor little soul with nothing you were left.

They was outcasts among the village people because they were Londoners.

Southwark pensioner

Evacuees returning to the Oliver Goldsmith School dispersal point in Peckham Road in June 1945. Evacuation ended on 7th September 1944.

2

There was quite a lull and I came home for a while. I was home for the January raid and that made me go away again. Then I went to a place where I had the most awful old lady that anybody could ever have. It was a great big house and she wouldn't have evacuees. It was compulsory, but that was against her grain. She didn't like me and she really made my life a misery. I wasn't allowed to wind the clock up. And you would have a flannel for this, and another flannel for that. And I never knew which was which, and she always used to stand there and watch me! And of course my children then were wearing 'siren' suits - all in one. She said it was disgusting for a little girl to have trousers on.

She wasn't very happy at all with us. Then my husband had leave, and she wouldn't let him stay with me. That was it. I went home to London.

Kathleen Ash

I think all of the children from Alexis Street School were evacuated to Worthing. We were put in the house of a retired civil servant, a Mr. Askey, whom we called Grandad - he was 68 - and his young looking 64 year-old wife who we said was much too young to be called Grandma, and anyway we had grandmas at home thank you. Anyway, we called her auntie. I remember trying to speak very poshly to Mr and Mrs Askey, trying to explain that Pat (my schoolfriend who was billeted with me) had no 'tail' in her pack, meaning that she had no towel. No one could understand a dicky-bird I was saying! They were absolutely wonderful to us.

'Grandad' was very traditionally English. We used to go into town with him every other Saturday to change our library books, get our hair cut for sixpence. We had the traditional fringes and short sides, children at that time. He took us

Christmas shopping. It was absolutely marvellous. He was very routine minded. I remember having syrup of figs every Friday night. In those days, hot water was quite difficult to achieve so it was only one bath a week but we had it regularly. Pat and I invented games like hide-and-seek on the landing upstairs which was a bit difficult for them really but we enjoyed it.

The people in Worthing were as kind as they could be. I had no feeling that we were outsiders in any way.

Doreen Woods

The whole school was totally disrupted by the fact that the London school was given the school buildings for the morning of one week and the afternoon of the next week and the Worthing children were shunted out into Parish Halls for the time they couldn't use the school. It was either the London school was in residence or the Worthing school was in residence.

Doreen Woods

The place I got in, she didn't really want us. I'm working like a skivvy in there - and yet they were getting paid for our keep. I was washing up, doing the dinner and everything. They were paid for our keep. There was two girls there and a father. Those girls weren't very nice to me because I was planted on them and they didn't seem to make me welcome. I said, 'I'm going home.' And I did.

Pensioner at the Yalding Centre

We used to go off into the fields. During the war, we used to get a fortnight off from school and we all had to go potato picking. We picked the potatoes and we got sixpence for that. I think it was for a week! It wasn't very much - it's quite hard work bending down picking up potatoes. Then we would get a week off for haymaking because most of the men had gone off to the war so they relied on the older children. We did haymaking and quite a bit of farmwork.

I loved it. I still keep friends with people we stayed with and I still go back to see them and I phone them every three months or so. I still like the country. Although I've come back and always lived in London, I did like it. It was lovely just to be able to roam down country lanes.

Doris Stevenson

48 Brandon Street
Walworth SE17
21st October 1941

Dear Nell,
Just a few lines in answer to your more than welcome letter. I was ever so pleased to hear from you. I wrote to you but I suppose our letters crossed in the post. Well dear, everybody's alright up to the time of writing. Nell, don't worry over me and don't think of coming home. It's very bad here and when I say so you know it is the truth because I don't make much of it. It was supposed to be a very quiet night last night, Monday, but when I came home this morning from the tube, I'm sorry to tell you that 76 Larcom Street, Mrs Miller's house and Mrs Kitchen's in Brandon Street were right down. Mrs Smith and Hilda Baylis's house in Charleston Street had been hit. Rodney Place, Rodney Road, Bronte Place, St Peters Church Liverpool Street, the crypt shelters under the church they say was faulting and Queen Street School is down and several other best of everything. It will all come right soon. So cheerio dear, good luck and God bless you and Doreen.

With fondest love and best wishes from your loving Mum and Dad.

BLACKOUT

Sandbags outside Abbey Buildings, Bermondsey Street in September 1939.

I made my own blackout. Got the big sheets and rolled them up and down. Made it like blinds. We were up at the top of the house, and we only used to have little candles, never had the lights on properly.

Mrs Quinlan

My sister and I were over the West End and when we were going along, the sirens went off. As we were running "Aah!" I bashed right into this shelter in the road. My legs! And my knee, the shins went right into them. You couldn't see, no. Nothing at all. I don't know how we got there.

Pensioner at the Yalding Centre

I can remember my sister-in-law and myself were walking along and we banged into a lamp-post. I thought it was just me that banged myself, but she was bleeding and I had a great big lump on my eyebrow. We both walked into the same post and didn't know!

Mary Clouter

It was like a thick black cardboard and we use to make frames and they used to fix them, very posh, you know. We used to get up in the morning and take them down and put them up again at night.

Queenie Turner

You'd get so bothered about it, you'd go round making sure there couldn't possibly be a chink of light, and you'd go outside and look right through, and yet the warden would say, "There's a chink of light there!" And I remember a squabble going on in two houses, where the man on the other side would just see this tiny chink - well it wasn't as big as a cigarette. I shouldn't think the Germans would ever see that! And he'd say, "Oh, you're going to end up in prison! I'm going to get the policeman!" Oh, the racket that went on, it was amazing, it really was... and you'd get so worried that you'd pin them with drawing pins that went all the way round the edge.

Grace Smith-Grogue

This area was devastated, no question about that, so when you started out, you didn't know how far you were going to get, because you didn't know what the problem was - if there was a hole in the road, or a burst gas main or water main, electricity up the wall, or whatever. So you couldn't gauge a journey - you couldn't say, "Well, it'll take me half an hour to get there", because you never knew, it could take you all day! But generally speaking, you could move around.

Lil Patrick

You'd just stick your tape diagonally across the windows. Anti-blast tape. Some of it was like a hessian tape. A lot of it was paper with very fine hessian lining. These were small Georgian windows so it was a bit expensive. The idea was that instead of the shards flying through, at least it would hold a lot of it in one piece, the broken panes. We had what they termed 'good quality blackout material,' which was something very much like leatherette. It was good quality stuff. We didn't need to change it once during the war. We had it on a roll. We used to roll it up manually. Then of a night time, pull it down and put drawing pins in the side to make sure that it was closed up. There wasn't supposed to be any light shining. Any little chinks of light and someone would go, "Put that light out!"

Bill Winter

I was coming home from work, and the blackout was on, and it was a dreadful fog, absolutely dreadful. And I got off the bus - now you could not see your own hand! And my torch gave out, and you could not see - it was just like a black curtain, and you felt your way. It was before the copings were taken away - because they took the railings for the war - so we had copings down where I lived. And if somebody had a torch, they would help you along. I'd say, "Where am I?" - because you wouldn't know whether you were across the road, that way. Absolutely that sticks in my mind, more than anything else, that particular night. It was ghastly! My sister was terrified, because I lived upstairs in her place, and she was waiting for me to come home. And then when I got to the turning, somebody said, "I think this is your turning," and I walked along, feeling my way. I knocked at three wrong doors before I found my own!

Bermondsey pensioner

Everybody was so kind. If you came along the road and it was blackout and people were there, they'd walk along with you. You never had any fear like you would today if you did it, even when the fogs was on. They'd walk along and some of the men in those days would say, "All right girl. Come along," and they'd walk along with you and we'd all walk along with any man that came along the road.

Doris Platt

We had some nice moonlit nights, which wasn't to our benefit because over would come the planes. There wasn't a lot of traffic. Bike lights, everything had a shade over the top. My sister lived down in Louth Road and I used to run down there to her in the blackout. You got used to it.

Mrs Bennett

One day I came back from Yorkshire for a week or two weeks. I came in and I forgot you had to black out everywhere. I had curtains. I could have done it easy, but I didn't. The Warden came up banging at the door and coming in and telling us, "Your light's shining out. We'll all get bombed." Being up in Yorkshire and never having to do it, I'd forgotten all about it and I didn't do it. Of course after that for a week or fortnight they just came up and did it for me. They was too scared that I'd forget, 'cause it was very serious.

Ivy Richardson

AIR RAIDS AND SHELTERS

We came back to London on the Saturday, the day after there was the worst raid on London. I thought the war was over, because the city was alight, the city was still alight from the night before. There was just burning buildings everywhere and it got worse and worse and then we crossed the river towards the Elephant and Castle - it was dreadful.

There were still fires going and there was masses of debris everywhere and it took you ages to walk through a street because you were going all over the bricks with your suitcases. When we got to my mother's house, the house had gone. It had been bombed with an oil bomb and there was just a shell as you walked in and the staircase standing, and nothing. I couldn't find my mother, but she'd been sent to a rest centre.

Doris Platt

We had a beautiful shop in Tower Bridge Road my grandfather built, it was called the Tower Bridge Palace. And in his cellar, which was a big cellar, he barricaded it all up, and made a great big door which we put up near the end and sand-bagged it. At night we all went down there. And lots of our neighbours went down there, and people who lived nearby, and relatives up the road. We had beds made out along the wall. And we lived down there, and in the morning we used to come out and have a look round, see what was missing. One day the house next door but one was gone, and we didn't hear it go in the night! I mean we heard these noises all night - crash, bang, wallop - but all you say is "that's near" or "that's far".

Joe Scala

It was just wide enough in our shelter for me to lay like widthways. But of course, anybody who came down... There was my sister, had a sailor man-friend and he was about 5'10", six foot. What happened to him: he had to lay one way and you had to put your legs over his legs. Most uncomfortable. You'd die for six o'clock to come, for the all-clear, for you to get out and either you fell into your bed for an hour or you had a bit of a wash down.

Grace Shelford

The Anderson shelter was all full of spiders and earwigs. We had a couple of bunks, you know, to sleep, but we hardly ever slept in there. It was horrible, believe me. There was four of us: Mum and Dad, my sister and myself. It was damp, you would get little creepy crawly spiders.

Pensioner at Kennington House

My Dad had the shelter all blocked out. He had all that oak panelling all the way round - he used to do carpentry as a hobby. We had beds down there, blankets, a little fire for cooking down there, an Aladdin paraffin stove. We had all different foods stored there, all tinned stuff so that if you had to stay down there for days and days you could. And you got a water butt down there. It was lovely.

May Roberts

Down the tube we used to enjoy ourselves, used to have a sing-song. Everybody was friendly and you used to make the best of it down there. All different turns, singing and that. They loved my little boy, specially when he was in his uniform. I don't know why we used to go to Piccadilly

Circus. I don't know if we tried to get in nearer or if that was perhaps the only one we could get. Course you got your own place and you kept your own things there.

Mrs Quinlan

Coming home from Peek Freans one day, walking along the road - I can still see it now, the Messerschmidts came right down, and all the children were coming out of school - it was in our dinner hour. As we came through that turning the children were coming out, we could hear these planes above us and they dive-bombed the railway bridge in Galleywall Road. We got all the children what we could and run them in the Victory Pub and put them under the table. But I could still see that pilot as he came right down, right onto the railway grinning. There was a helmet but you could see the grin on his face, that's how low he came. There was all the bullet holes all along the bridge.

Emily Lane

At Crosse and Blackwell's in Crimscott Street where I worked, they used to make us go down the shelter. But we lost such a lot of time that afterwards, when the raids wasn't so bad we worked 'till it got near, then they put us down the shelters. They had spotters on the roof and when the air raids were announced they'd watch the planes. When they got too near, they'd sound the alarm and we all went down to the shelters till the all-clear went. If it was dinner -time we'd run home.

Doris Stevenson

The devastation of Barrow, Hepburn and Gales leather manufacturers, in Grange Road, May 1941.

There was a rocket hit us. There was never any warning. Everything in our booking office where I worked, everything collapsed and all the tickets... It was a terrible mess. The first thing you knew was, you heard the explosion and then everything about you just collapsed. There was tickets everywhere. It was a muddle. You are just trembling and you don't know what's going on. They just came and put you in a car and take you to a depot and give you something and see that you're alright.

Ivy Richardson

And then in the morning when it was light we used to go out in the garden and pick up the bombs, the incendiary bombs. Some were blasted but some were not. My brothers used to throw them at one another laughing. It was dangerous. You wasn't allowed to keep them really.

May Roberts

My sister and sister-in-law's husband and his sister and whole family were all killed. They had got home on leave - he got married in the day time - and then they were all in the club in the night time all singing and dancing, then an air raid alert came on so they went down into the public shelter in Camberwell there. A land mine came on. If they had stayed in the pub they would have been alright. They were just all killed. The whole family got wiped out.

Mary Clouter

Alexander's, the timber yard was all ablaze. It was a blasting bomb, like a land mine type of bomb. It blew the shelters out of the ground, over the wall, into the canal. Not all of them - the ones down the other end of the road, fortunately, from where we were. And these shelters - I remember seeing them floating in the canal. Some people were killed there. A lot of people just had their clothes blown off. Their clothes were completely blown off and they were naked. I saw one little girl who came along who had nothing on. They took my coat and wrapped it round her. It was my new coat - blue, and it had a blue hat. They took this coat off of me and wrapped it round her. She was okay, very shaken but not a mark on her. Just all her clothes were blown off of her. It's amazing.

We all went down to Spa Road arches. Our family knew 10-15% of the people that went in, personally. There were bunk beds - lower, middle, upper. As kids we would be sitting on top watching everything, to make sure that you could see above everybody else. It was a tremendous experience. It was like going up to the pictures and seeing your hero getting the best of whoever.

Bill Winter

My father had gone out into the shelter in Donaghue Estate and was coming back to the post. He'd just come out of Donaghue Estate down onto the pavement in Fort Road and he said it was blinding. He said all you heard was a heavy "Pheeeew." There was a big blinding white flash and the whole building shook in front of his eyes and started crumbling. Next thing was, he came to when they were pulling him out of the drain cover where he'd been blown by the blast, up over the railings. They hadn't taken the railings away. They were about five foot six tall. They'd blown him right the way up and he had landed about forty foot away from where he had originally started. He lived. He came down on an inspection plate, on one of the covers. Smashed it. He was head and shoulders down the drain when they found him.

Bill Winter

If we woke up in the night and we didn't have time to get down to the shelter or Dad thought it might not be a big heavy raid, we'd get under the table.

May Roberts

It was October 25th 1940, and my brother was out with his friends and they went into the local billiard hall which was also being used as a shelter with lots and lots of families in there that hadn't been evacuated. And the bomb came in through the railway line. I think 190 were killed that night. He was one that was injured. But he was unconscious and burnt, and it took us three days to find him because his identity card and driving licence and all those kind of things were stolen out of his jacket pocket. They probably used them for illegal purposes.

On the same night, our house - it wasn't bombed, but the blast had made it unusable, and so there was no way of securing it. And in the corner there was a bookcase, and my mother's brothers and sisters were clever and they'd had prizes from school. And one of the books was Walter Scott's novels, and each illustration had tissue paper over it, and it was beautifully bound. And that bookcase just disappeared with all its contents.

Lil Patrick

AIR RAID PRECAUTIONS

We had to fire-watch once a month. I'm afraid we enjoyed ourselves when we had to fire-watch because it wasn't very far from a pub - there was two girls and about four of the men had to do it. We used to shoot up to the pub and all sit up there and when a siren went we all had to rush down.

Doris Platt

There were a lot of fire and incendiary bombs at that time, a lot of them. And we had a rota for night duty, to watch.

You dumped them in buckets of sand. I can remember going out onto a flat roof with all these buckets, and putting out the incendiaries. Apart from fire-watching, we played table tennis! There was table tennis in the Town Hall - in the Council Chamber. I was keen on table tennis. I can remember all the seats around it! After that, they put it in the basement, but it wasn't so good - we liked the atmosphere in the Council Chamber! And as long as somebody was watching, you could play table tennis, and then have your turn at watching.

There were about ten of us per night, watching for bombs. And if there were more than we could cope with, then we had to phone to get some assistance.

Edna Davis

I remember it. I was on ARP. There was a shop on the corner of our road, a laundry. We used to sleep on the racks of the shop. Because we had to be on duty, you see. We thought it was great fun.

Southwark pensioner

I was supposed to do fire-watching, but my husband got me out of that. He said I wasn't doing it. Why should I look after other people's property? I didn't do it.

Ethel Cadge

I was a telephonist, sending out the services you know, the police, to rack off the area and whatever was required, the rescue, the fireman and the van that collected the dead bodies. It could be rather gruesome really. You had to take an exam for it. I loved it. I didn't want the war to go on for ever, but the companionship among us was great.

Pensioner at Kennington House

Whenever the warning went, we had to report. Whether it was our turn on duty or not, we all turned up. You were all available. The rest of the time you had duty rotas, so that there was always a presence there. And this was in the early hours of the morning. My patch was Tooley Street, around the foot of Tower Bridge, around the wharves and around that area, and I was standing in the shelter at the block of Devon Mansions - flats in Tooley Street which are still there - and we saw this thing come over. It was making this dreadful noise and we saw it come over, and we said, "Three cheers, that's one we've got!" - thinking it was an aircraft that had been brought down by anti-aircraft fire, and it went on and on. And it took from that time, which was the early hours of the morning, until about mid-afternoon before we actually found out what it was that was happening to us. Yes, it was quite frightening.

Lil Patrick

Where I worked, we would leave off work at 5 o'clock and sign on at 5.30 for fire-watching. It came a turn around every ten days and we split it because it was a big building and there was eight on each fire watching. We had little beds. It was a nuisance sleeping there all night when they were sending bombs down, but if your turn came around you had to turn up on a Sunday night as well.

Mrs Ward

Going back one day, walking towards the Elephant when we lived in Peckham, during the night there'd been a really heavy raid, bombs were dropping all round. I walked along towards the New Kent Road, along Old Kent Road. I turned the corner there, and there's two buses, one with its front up against the wall and the other one was on its side. There was wardens and ambulances. The ambulances they used weren't like today's ambulances, they were just vans with a sheet over them. One was just pulling them down, others were loading up people. The one that was just pulling away, a fella there had got another body he wanted to put on. He said, "Another one here Charlie." He said, "Sorry. Full up. Be back in a minute." I carried on walking down towards the Elephant. You just took it in your stride. It was happening so much all around you that you took it as a natural thing almost.

Southwark pensioner

I think all through the war you will find this: most people will say the mothers were the focal point. My Dad didn't go into the army but he spent most of the war either fire-spotting or on warden patrol. Your mother was the one, and your grandmother. Grandmothers were a great mainstay. I view my grandmother with great affection because she was our second mother, you might as well say. Although we saw Dad, he was a fleeting figure at times because he'd come in and he'd have his shave and after a night of being out patrolling the sector of bombing he'd be off to work. By the time he came home in the evening, we were packed off down the shelter to go to sleep again.

Doreen Davis

The worst bombing was Stainer Street arch. I had a relation who was on the Rescue, he was a civilian. He was too old to go in the army, he was a foreman on the Council. They made them rescue people who were bombed out. He was never right for two or three months after what he saw in there. Where you get the railway arches, Stainer Street and Druid Street, there was all people in there because it was a shelter. The bomb went right through first and then exploded inside. It was all arms and legs all over the place. He was really bad for two or three months with shock. It is well known amongst old Bermondsey people because hundreds got killed in there. They reckoned nearly everybody in Abbey Street lost somebody.

Joe French

In the daytime I worked in a bank in the City, and at night time, after I was registered, I was put in the fire service, for nights. I didn't go out - I was in the control room, sending the others out. I thought it was a bit hard actually, because I had to stay on the phone all night and the crews all went into the shelter in the garden. I had to sit in control. And if you had any trouble they had these little 'Green Goddess' fire engines - it was a sort of van, green.

Jeanne Quick

I got a job on the Council as an ambulance driver because there was a man away on holiday. I remember going to Guinness's buildings in Page's Walk. I was supposed to stay with the lorry. There was a huge bomb dropped there. So I went in, I don't know what floor it was on - it's so long ago - and there was a woman sitting by the fire with a little baby, looking at the baby. I said, "Come on lady, you can come out now. It's more or less clear." They were dead. The shock. Like that. And her husband - this is true - was embedded in the wall. The blast had - right in the wall. As they pulled him out all his clothes and flesh was left on the wall.

Leonard Whitlock

I wasn't called up. I was more or less 'reserved' working for the public utilities. I was working on the London Fire Brigade. On the outbreak of war I was putting extra appliances in school buildings because the Fire Brigade then moved into the schools permanently. They appealed for volunteers. You went to the headquarters and then you got posted. I joined as a volunteer and I went to New Cross Fire Station. In addition to that I used to do fire watching on the Gas Company's show-rooms. Then I had to join the Home Guard. So it was quite busy really.

Mr Samson

My uncle was in the Auxiliary Fire Service, and we made a game of when a fire bomb dropped, to get there and put it out within ten seconds - you had to get on your hands and knees, crawl, get there within ten seconds, put a sandbag on it and run away. And then if it exploded, that would kill the explosion... I done that twice, twice I did that. And I'll never forget. I cut a very heroic figure once, because Bermondsey in those days, you could smell Bermondsey. When you got near Bermondsey, there was three smells: you could smell Hartley's jam factory during the day time - beautiful, oh, this beautiful strawberry jam being made! - and a biscuit factory, Huntley and Palmers biscuit factory. But all day long, the pervading smell of leather; it was an area where leather was being tanned. And the other smell was vinegar. Up near Tower Bridge there was a big vinegar distillery, Sarsons I think, and you could smell that. And we used to go out at night and we used to have these adventures, and dash about and do all these things; and one night there was a couple of girls with us, and I thought, "Right now, this is my big chance!" and I charged off to do something brave in Bermondsey! And it was all dark - there was no lights on except fires burning, and then I ran across the road, and as I ran, I suddenly disappeared, and I put my foot in a thing where the firemen got the water from to put the fires out - the hydrant thing. And I put my foot down there, and I had a wellington on and it got all full up with water and it ruined my night! Everyone was laughing, so I had to try something else to impress the girls.

Joe Scala

Civil Defence training in 1940: how to put out a fire.

FOOD AND RATIONING

You joined a queue, and you didn't know what you were queuing for sometimes! Everybody joined a queue.

Deborah Playne

If ever you saw a queue, you joined in - you didn't know what it was you were queuing for.

Iris Wilkins

Over the road there was a beautiful veg and fruit shop, Michael's. Their girl, the middle girl that was the same age as my David, they used to go up to school together. They got very friendly and he liked her and she liked him. She used to say to David, "Tell your mum that Dad's having the oranges in tomorrow". So I knew before anybody else knew, the day to go up and you lined up and you could get things. That's how we existed. We just had to.

Ivy Richardson

The messages used to go around, you know, "They've got bananas down there, and oranges up here! You're only allowed one!", and then the queue would form, and you'd have this long queue. The fish queue - that really was something! You can imagine the shortage of fish. Groves', down near St James' Church - "He's having fish in this morning" - so you'd get in the queue. And it could be miles long! And you'd move along slowly as he sold the fish, and probably, by the time it got to your turn, that was the last, and you were just too late. You'd stood there for a couple of hours, you know, and there was no fish left!

Lil Patrick

We used to have corned beef sausages and pork pies that my father used to sell in the shop. Once we was indoors and my Dad came down and said, "There's a bit of meat for you. Put this meat in the oven." So Mother put the meat in the oven. He sort of had this look and he said, "We've got a bit extra this week. I don't know how." Anyhow she put this meat in the oven and she'd just about got it ready to put in when the street doorbell went. When he went and opened the street door this lady said, "I haven't had my rations this week." Well, father got the meat out and off she went with it. We ended up with corned beef.

Member of Southwark Pensioners group

Opposite where I lived there used to be a very nice shop where they sold butter and eggs and things and I didn't get the egg ration which I thought I should. The eggs were in but I wasn't getting mine. And when I asked her about them, sort of insisted, she was being a bit funny - "Smash yours when I get them." And I said, "And I'll smash your face for you as well." But on the whole you didn't get temperish.

Mrs Quinlan

I think we got better food in as much as that you could always go in and get a cooked breakfast, even if it was only egg on toast, or some streaky bacon. I don't think the civilians could do that - their rations never ran to it. And there was always a sweet! I'm sure the civilians never had enough food to have a sweet everyday. So I think we were better fed.

Mary Gibson

Girls from Southwark Central School gardening while evacuated to Newton Abbot, Devon. They are being visited by Mr Davies, Chairman of the London County Council.

They dug up the grass outside our flats and they said we could have an allotment and people had these terrific allotments so we decided we were going to have one. So we had this square outside our bedroom and we put carrots in and different things in and then we was playing a game one day and we decided to play cooking, so we dug up all the carrots and ate them!

Member of Irish Club at Amigo Hall

I had an aunty living in Guildford who we visited from time to time, just to keep in touch. You know, eggs appeared, and they used to keep chickens. It was great to have an egg - you thought you were really.... it was luxury!

Then when we worked over at Highbury, we had to go into the cafe for our dinner. We had baby's head - that's what they called it. And it was a little individual meat pudding, it was made from bullock's cheek. And we had rice with custard on it. You know, all the men used to come in and shout out, "baby's head and two!" That's meat pudding and two veg.

Lil Patrick

I used to go up every Saturday to Nunhead, and walk up and back, and queue up to get horsemeat. Horse flesh. We had it. It was quite nice! They didn't know what I was feeding them!

Nell Todd

You used to share. If you had a friend, say they didn't like eggs, you'd give them tea and they'd give you their eggs or vice versa. Or you'd buy them off them. I knew a girl worked at a tea factory so we used to get tea alright, see? I used to pay her rent for her! She used to go to work in the daytime and couldn't pay her rent, so I'd do it for her. Then when she come out, she'd give me the tea. That's how we worked it.

Flo Ball

My father worked at the Times and the News of the World. He could fetch home white paper that hadn't been printed on. My father used to come back on the Sunday morning and take the paper round to Edwards, 'cause they couldn't get it. It was all cut in squares, it was marvellous. So every now and again my dad got a leg of lamb for that.

Ivy Richardson

We were close to the docks, and we always considered this to be the larder of London, so you had a hell of a lot of dockers working in and out of there, and they weren't all choir boys by any means! And many a case has been dropped, and you know, "Sorry about that, it slipped!" And so there was a little source of supply coming through there, which was kept very quiet!

Bill Gibson

We were lucky because when we were in Yorkshire, near to us was this farm. Their daughters were all that bit older so they wanted clothes but they didn't have the coupons. My mother having four children couldn't afford to spend all her coupons, she hadn't got the money to spend so we had coupons to spare. What we used to do was, we gave the people clothing coupons and from the farm they used to give us back butter which they'd made and stuff. When they went and bought material and they had made their clothes, whatever bits they had left they made into dresses for us.

Doris Stevenson

We did get our wedding cake made, because we knew somebody who made a lovely fruit cake for us, and almonds I think. But there was no icing sugar, so we had a cardboard covering. Everyone did! With all little bits and pieces on it. And it looked so real that when we were going to cut the wedding cake, everyone went "Aaaah..."

Grace Smith-Grogue

I used to send the children round for sausages. I used to get however many they would allow you. Sometimes you'd get a pound, sometimes you'd only get about six. Once I sent my two, and my eldest one got his and the other one was only about five and she said to him, "I've just served your brother," so he didn't get any and he came home crying. She knew it was him. I was trying to work the oracle, trying to get two lots.

Mrs Bennett

It was word of mouth. They would come along and say, "Mrs that, her daughter works at so-and-so's - she can get you bacon." If you had the money to pay, then you'd tell Mrs so-and-so who then told Mrs so-and-so and the bacon would come down the trail. If you had the money I think you probably could get most things, if you could afford to get it. Of course a lot of people couldn't, so they didn't.

Doris Stevenson

You had to get fuel where you could. There was a place down by Rotherhithe Tunnel - a gasworks - where you could get the coke. Then of course you had to have something - push chairs or whatever you could get - to wheel it home, because it was about a mile away. Then there was a little shop where coal used to be delivered from time to time. And the message would go round - "Maggie's got coal! Take the push chair round!" And so we'd get in the queue and we'd get our bag of coal. And it was thick snow, and of course the stuff we had on the push-chair far out-weighed what the push-chair could take, and pushing it across the snow didn't help! So there we were with the wheels gradually going out like this! And we ended up by dispensing with the push-chair, and pulling the coal along in the sack on our way home, sliding it along the ground. And if there was bomb damage anywhere and there were beams, wood, or whatever, you'd get the push-chair round there, and load the beams on there, and then bring it home and saw it all up.

Lil Patrick

I worked at Crosse and Blackwell's on baked beans. I used to label them. If we got one and it was bent, had something wrong with it, we used to put that in a certain place and it would be sold in our shop, the factory shop. People who worked at Crosse and Blackwell's could buy stuff in there cheap, like a tin of salmon you could get for six pence a tin. You got them cheap because they couldn't sell them. Some of them they did sell actually. There was a man who used to be in a little shop in the Old Kent Road. He'd buy a lot of damaged stock, jam from Hartley's, beans from Crosse and Blackwell's, and sell them cheap.

Flo Ball

One day this old boy turns up with a big shoebox full of clothing coupons. So he said, " Want these?" for a tanner each or something, so I said, "Alright, I'll have them." So I did, we were all fiddling you know. And anyway, I gave some to an aunt of mine, who was a very well respected lady, and she used to shop in very expensive shops like Jones and Higgins, beautiful shops in those days, with the floor walker and morning dress and everything. And she phoned me one day, and she said, "Oh, could you come and see me," she said, "I've bought some curtains" or something, she said, "and he says they're not real coupons at all." Oh Christ, I thought. I said, "Well, just tell her, look just tell her that somebody borrowed some coupons from her, when they were short of coupons, to get something, and when he had to pay her back, he'd paid her back with coupons and they were the coupons he'd paid her. But he was in the airforce and he's gone to sea now and he's gone somewhere." So you know, they didn't worry. It went on all the time.

Joe Scala

They were very nice dresses. You'd have one colour for the bodice and the sleeves would be a different colour and the collar was different. Not all patchwork - the two sleeves matched in colour but were a different colour, the pockets were a different colour. We used to have all these creations left from the adult clothes made into clothes for us. We used to have skirts - one bit was skirt and the top was made like a blouse. If it didn't meet for the blouse, they'd let in another bit so it looked as if you had a strap. Beautifully done.

Doris Stevenson

When the parachutes used to come down, they used to crash, my friend and I used to go and buy the parachutes silk and make our clothes out of them. My friend made her bridal outfit out of that.

Emily Lane

The Yanks would bring stockings but I didn't know any Yanks. You were lucky to know somebody who knew somebody, sort of thing. I had a couple of pairs of stockings from America, I think. My husband would forage round.

Mrs Bennett

We can't survive without a cup of tea, you know. I suppose it's like the French with wine. The first thing we do when we've got a problem is to get the kettle on, so the amount of tea that was allocated to us was obviously insufficient. And this is how it was done: people you knew, friends, would say, "I can get my hands on some tea if you want!" I can't remember the prices now, but it was always twice as much. And that was obviously stolen from somewhere, wasn't it? I mean it had to be, didn't it, when you stopped to think about it. But you know, the moral side of it, when you're gasping for a cup of tea, you kind of put that in the grey area don't you, and think, "No that wasn't me - I didn't do that!", but we did. We all did it.

Lil Patrick

The National Emergency Washing Service provided a mobile launderette for the waterless residents of East Surrey Grove in May 1943.

WORK IN WAR

I worked for a firm in Abbey Street. When the raids started, we used to do the bomb damage. When all the windows got blown out we would put the black stuff up to stop the light coming in the window. You'd see a roof smashed right in. Just repaired it and a week later it got all blown up again.

Many times there was a raid while you were working. You took no notice of it. Everybody got used to bombing and it never worried people that much.

Joe French

At the start of the war I was working in Surrey Docks as a deal porter. Surrey Commercial Docks was huge. All ships used to come in from Russia, Finland and Sweden with timber. I never believed that Surrey Commercial Dock would close for timber. Then they bombed the docks in 1940 and there was a vast fire. They never opened any more really. Not for deal portering. Well, you had to earn a living. I was married and had got a child. I'd got to earn money. So I went to the Labour Exchange and they sent me to Guildford building tank traps.

Leonard Whitlock

It was a case of - you went into the forces or you did munitions work. I went and was trained as an engineer. An engineer takes seven years to train, doesn't he? I was given three months.

You worked seventy hours a week, from seven at night till seven in the morning. I must tell you - I was quite good at this lathe, doing a two star thread - very nerve racking. Not a lot of people could do it. It was for the tail pins of the aeroplanes to turn doubly quick. You dealt in millimetres I think - thousandths. You used to go in and the lathe would turn. Now you had to pull it out to go back, but you had to remember where you went in. You had to know how far out you'd pulled it, 'cause if you didn't pull it out far enough you'd take your screw right off straight away. You had a wheel here and you would drop in your tool, bring it out, go back, put it in a thousandth or whatever you wanted to take off again, wait till the wheel come round to six and drop in again. I was the head girl at that factory.

Grace Shelford

In the Town Hall there were lots of people. But later on it was mainly girls, because the men were called up. But when I worked there to begin with, there were three girls and two hundred boys, so you can imagine...! And they were called up, and so you had the girls from the libraries that were closed down during the war - you see, Dulwich Library was bombed, so the girls from there had to come to the Town Hall.

My friend and I volunteered to begin with, to join the Land Army. After all, the boys had been sent off, it wasn't the same in the Town Hall, so we thought we'd join up. But the council said no; they wouldn't release us to join up. And then later we decided we'd try for nursing, and they said, "Yes, you can join up as long as you don't train," because they got the feeling that we wouldn't come back if we trained. It was a bit silly really.

Because my husband was invalided out of the forces, I was released. I only had to do a part-time job - you know, you were directed, during the war. So I got a part-time job in the library and I thought this was fine, but the local Council said, "You haven't been directed to this job. You have no right to get a job on your own!" So they directed me to a builders' office, doing the book-keeping.

Edna Davis

Well I was called up. They said that I had to go in the forces, because I had no children. So I said, "Oh, I don't want to go into the forces", as I had a husband. So they said, "Well, then you must get a job doing war work." So I went and made Anderson shelters. Well I stuck that for a little while, then I thought, well this is not for me, it's too heavy! So I applied to be a tram conductress, but I don't know whether that was worse - I suppose it was - but I did have a nice driver; he used to meet me at four o'clock in the morning, you know. I had to get on the tram then. We had no training, but you did anything you had to.

Milly Jackson

At sixteen, I worked in the motive power department at Plaistow on the railway engines, the big steamers. We were cleaning the engines then. There was a shortage of manual labour, the men being away, so we was out in next to no time, firing these engines at sixteen, sixteen-and-a-half years old. Ruddy great... it was no good playing about. You had to do the procedures, what the fireman had to do. You was taught how to do that. You had to clean the fire. You got a six foot fire there. You've got to clean it out. It's red hot, clinkers and everything. You'd bring this big lump of clinker out on the end of the shovel - you're only sixteen - and you throw it out through the gap there on the engine. You've only got a bit of cloth there. Everything is red hot. I saw this boy, same age as me, he came from Tilbury, and as he threw the clinker, he's caught the end of the shovel and it bounced right back on his hand. He was taken over to Plaistow Hospital General. This is what the kids of the day had to do, at sixteen years old.

Ron Kendrick

The medical superintendent said, "Ladies and Gentlemen, today we invaded Normandy. Will you go back to your wards, and get ready for patients please." It was very strange to me to find that they arrived in our hospital, which was some way from the coast, and they were all still in their wet uniforms. I didn't think, really. I somehow thought somebody would look after them and dry them before they got to us. But they were still wet where they had been picked off the beaches. I know one thing - we didn't nurse the Americans and the British too close together. We put the British one end of the ward and the Americans at the other. They didn't get on very well.

Joan Piper

I went back to work when my eldest one was about two, two and a half, and I had him in a nursery. They had things to play with, and they had a paddling pool. He was quite happy there, I think. And many a time I got off the bus and went into a shelter on the way to work - with him! - and then I've gone back when the all-clear went, got to work 10 or 11 o'clock. I was working in a uniform factory. That was in Tooley Street, near London Bridge.

Florence Spike

There was a feeling that you were all in it together, wherever you were. I worked in a factory close by a railway and that factory was bombed the same week as we were bombed out of our home. So I was without a job, without a home, and that went on for about six weeks until we found somewhere to live. I was working for a leather firm - we were nearly all in the leather industry around here.

We were making Sam Brown Belts, and leather cases that the electricians used to keep their gear in. They found another place down by the wharves, and moved in there; very temporarily, because we were burnt out there shortly afterwards. And then off we went to Highbury on a short lease. From Highbury, we were moved to Chalk Farm, to a part of the Chappell's piano factory - they weren't making pianos anymore, so we had space. You know, we were a bit like nomads. But having to get yourself to Chalk Farm from Bermondsey in war time was no joke.

Lil Patrick

I taught in London. We had one class in the morning and one class in the afternoon. Then in the September when the blitz started we were transferred to rest centre work and I was in a big school off the Old Kent Road. We did 24 hours on, 24 hours off, 120 hours a fortnight, in two teams. I must say we got wonderful co-operation from the people that were being bombed out. You get good community spirit when something like that happens. But it was a very bad area. I don't think a night went by without some trouble in the area.

Elsie Blenkey

My parents wouldn't let us join the services - my father especially, so I volunteered for the Land Army. I went as a driver. I hadn't driven before except I'd had a go in my father's car, but not really on the roads.

Well, I remember feeling quite chuffed, really, in the first uniform I was given, because that was corduroy breeches, and a sort of cowboy hat! And when I arrived at the training centre, everybody laughed at me - they said, "You won't last long like that! That's not your working gear!" They were quite right, and it was dungarees from then on.

We used to work ninety hours a week. You moved around to different farms. We were sort of contract workers, I think they'd call them today - contract gangs. And we used to move all around the farms in Buckinghamshire, and on the borders of Bedfordshire. I used to drive this van, I was chauffeur and forewoman. I got seventeen shillings a week but out of that we had to pay our lodgings.

Apart from driving the tractor, I did ploughing, harvesting, hay-making, potato picking with a spinner - that's the worst job out of the lot, because you spun them out of the ground, but then you had to pick them up, and that was on all fours, so by the time you got to the end of the row... that was horrible work.

Ivy Maylan

Ivy Maylan and fellow Land Army girls.

We had to go in one at a time and be interviewed. It came my turn, and he said, "What would you like to do? Why do you want to join the Air Force?" I said, "Well I've always wanted to join the Air Force." And then he said, "Well, what do you want to do?" I said, "Well, to tell you the truth, I want to do something for the war, but I never want to kill anyone!" So he said, "Well, cook!" so I said, "You've never tasted my cooking!" I'm 18 and a half, 19, remember and I'm talking to this man with all this gold braid on him, and he says, "Well, general duties." I said, "What does that entail?" He said, "Well, sweeping and ....." Well I said, "No, that's not what I want. I want something exciting!" and behind him on the wall, there was this beautiful, magnificent motorboat jumping out of the sea, and it was an RAF rescue launch, and I said, "Actually, that's what I wanted to do, I've always wanted to do that." So he said, "Well, that's very difficult. It's a very, very small unit, and there's only a few scattered here and there these boats, it's not like big aerodromes of them, you just live in a house and put the boats out and put them to sea." So I said, "That's what I really want to do." "Well, you seem very keen," he said, "but I must tell you that in this section, the marine section, are these sons of millionaires who've been brought up on yachts all their life and know everything about it, all these young fellas, or stevedores off the River Thames, the bargees who have served five years apprenticeship and can handle boats." He said, "I can see you are eager, so couldn't you just tell me, are you in any-way loosely connected with the sea? Just loosely, you know, I'm just trying to help you, just loosely!" So I said, "Yes I am." He said, "How's that then?" I said, "Well my dad's got a fish and chip shop!" So he took his cap off and mopped his forehead, and looked at the officer next to him, and he said, "What do you think?" And this other officer said to him, "He sounds like ideal material to me!" So that's how I joined the Air Force - the Air Sea Rescue. And it was really marvellous, you know, four and a half years I was on the sea, exciting action all the time.

Joe Scala

I was in the mixed heavy attack battery in the WRACs. I used to be what they used to call a height-finder - that was finding the height and distance of the target. But you couldn't stay on the doodle-bug, because it was going too fast. But if they did plod, yes you'd fire at them, but I can't say that I ever remember our battery hitting the target. I think it was the aircraft that got them.

Our discipline was very strong. If you got the evening off, and you went out to the pub, if you came back at one minute past twelve, you were on a charge. And also, they were very strict about the men keeping to their huts, and us keeping over the other side of the road in our huts. But you wouldn't do anything outrageous, because you were too afraid. I was put on a charge once; I didn't get back in time. Instead of being in at one minute to twelve, I was in at quarter past twelve, I think. I think I'd been home because my mum had got blasted out, and the trains were all up the wall, so I didn't get back to camp till quarter past. But I lost three days' pay for that quarter of an hour - which was a lot of money when you were only getting seven shillings a week. So that made you make sure you got in on time. We accepted it. It was all accepted. You took orders, you did as you were told, and if you were put on a charge, you'd done something wrong and you accepted it.

Mary Gibson

I've got cuttings from the newspaper at that time where the British government have asked the people from the colonies to volunteer. Try and remember that Britain was at war and Britain could not have beat the Germans on their own.

I remember arriving at Greenock from Jamaica. It was a cold November and it was snowing and all that. It was dirty grey. The Salvation Army came on the troop ship train and gave you a cup of tea and a bun. There were not that many people about but the people that you did see welcomed you because they was at war and you came to help. When I eventually got to the camp, we were all welcomed in the community because we were needed.

Sam King

I was in the concert party in the Air Force. We was in a little squad on our own and we used to go and entertain wherever they wanted us. And guard duty and all that. What I did towards the war was.....nil!

Leonard Whitlock

I can remember hearing the bombs, D-Day, you know when they went over there, and I remember the soldiers crying. They didn't want to go, I can remember that.

They said so, well they knew they were going overseas but they didn't know anything about D-Day, and they were doing assault courses you know, and some of them couldn't swim.

Eleanor Ala

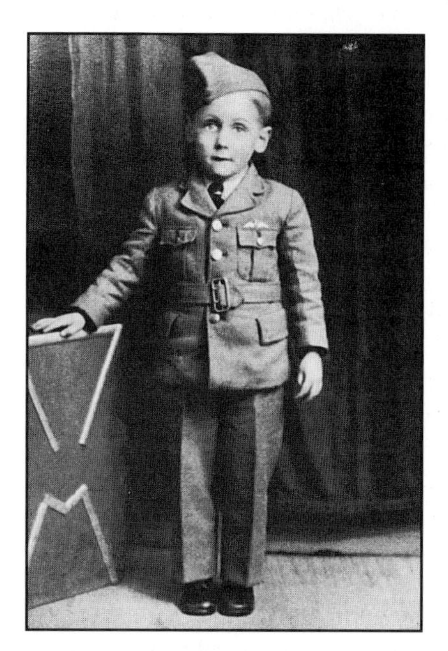

Above: Denis Quinlan age 4 in 1941. This uniform was purchased from Whitehall clothiers, Walworth Road.

Left: Sam King as a RAF Corporal then stationed at RAF Sealand near Chester.

When you see your mates joining up and going off, you don't want to be left out. I never volunteered, mind you, but I said, "When my time comes, I'll go in." Which I did.

I was in the bomb disposal squad. That was a regiment that was formed during the war. It never existed at the beginning of the war. They asked for volunteers but they didn't get any. It was "You, you and you" and that's it. I'm no hero! I didn't volunteer for it! I just happened to be standing too much to the front.

Joe Seeley

Of course all the people along the Irish coast, the majority of men along the coast line was in the Navy, even joined the British Navy and Air Fleet Arm, the Air Force. That was because they wanted to venture, young men - it was an adventure. Well it was hardly surprising. An awful lot of the young boys went from Ireland to England to fight the war. Although you think there is a lot of friction between England and Ireland, there isn't really, not from the South. England was bred into us really, wasn't it? I mean there was even men there who was in Irish Guards over here who lived in Ireland but were in the Irish Guards in England and that was even before the war. A lot of men are soldiers of fortune as they say - a lot of Irish people went to the war for England, they just joined up.

Stella Scanlon

He volunteered. He used to be a home guard, with the other boys, in the Drill Hall. Then he went and volunteered and put his age up. My dad tried to get him back. You're not supposed to go overseas before you're eighteen. He was about three months off of eighteen. My dad wrote to the commanding officer but they couldn't do nothing about it because he had volunteered. If he had been called up that would have been a different matter. We didn't know until he got home. He came home and said, "I've joined up." I can remember, I was only young, see? Mum started crying 'cause he was her favourite. He said, "I've joined the army." "No, no!" 'Cause my brother had gone in the Royal Artillery, in front of him, 'cause he was about 4 years older than him, so he'd gone. He was called up and he went, and course he wanted to go in it 'cause his brother was in it.

"To my dear Mother.
Though distant seas keep us apart,
Fondest thoughts of you are in my heart.
And so dear mother do not pine,
For the storm will soon be over and once
more the sun will shine."

And there's a ship on the picture and it says, "To hands across the sea." My brother wrote that to my mother just before he died in May 1944. He got drowned out in Burma. He was eighteen and a half.

They got a telegram. My mum used to do office cleaning. She came home at lunchtime. Course my dad had come home from work. She broke her heart. She got pneumonia. She went all round. We used to have great big tubs full up with water, called them water tanks, what the firemen used to put their hose in for the water. My mum went all looking in the water tanks calling for our Eddie. His name was Eddie. All over Tower Bridge. A policeman picked her up. He said, "What's the matter?" She said, "My son's drowned." He said, "Where?" She said, "In the water." She's walking around the water tanks, looking in the water tanks thinking he was in there. She come home and she had that pneumonia and she was bad for about three months. I was about eight or nine at the time.

May Roberts

HAVING A GOOD TIME

When servicemen came home on leave there was always a party for them somewhere or other.

Pensioner at Kennington House

We used to go dancing at the Lyceum in the West End, it was two shillings. And Covent Garden, I always remember Covent Garden. That's where they have the opera. But they had it open for dancing. It was big and it used to be two shillings in the afternoon, just for the afternoon. And there was evening dancing too. I'd get the tube and walk home from the Elephant and everywhere there were searchlights going, but we seemed to just do it.

Ethel Dorney, Sabina Brooks

I'm not saying that we weren't frightened. We used to go dancing at the Astoria, Charing Cross Road in Covent Garden. We used to go to the Locarno, Streatham. And you used to come out of there at half past eleven at night and catch the 133 bus or tram to the Elephant. No thought of, "Will I be all right?" Sometimes you would go in the Milk Bar and have a milk shake. At half eleven, walk down Tooley Street down to where I lived. Not by myself - there used to be four boys who lived over at Stamford Hill way. Don't ask me how they got to Stamford Hill, but they used to come to Streatham and to London Bridge and walk down Tooley Street and then they would have to get back. I don't know how they got back. I'm looking back and sometimes you were very frightened. But on the whole you think, "Very nice" - the feeling of safety and being able to walk about the streets and never any fear that way. I don't know why.

Grace Shelford

I'd missed the last train home to Dulwich, and sitting on the station, very forlorn - because you couldn't get taxis either, you know, there was no petrol for taxis. Almost in tears because I thought my parents were going to kill me, my father was going to be absolutely furious if I wasn't in by a certain time. And the station master came up; he said, "What's the trouble, miss?" so I told him. So he said, "Well, I'll tell you what, there's an engine coming along in a minute, and if you'd like to go back, you can go back on the engine." I can never remember being so terrified - it was worse than the bombing - because it was a steam engine, and you had to climb up about...well it seemed about fifty feet, in high heels! And he said, "Sit on that ledge," which was about that wide, you know, and you're clinging on, and as you're dashing through the dark, all the steam and the sparks are flying back at you. And it was quite horrifying.

Ivy Maylan

As kids you would play normal games. Tippy Cat: that was played with two pieces of wood. You have a small piece on the pavement. You hit it with a bigger stick, hit it up in the air and try and hit it as far away as you could. It is rather like rounders without a ball. You didn't need a ball. All you needed was two pieces of wood.

Tin Tang Copper: two teams would part up. The idea was to hide. There was a tin and a couple of pieces of wood. You throw them. They've got to assemble the tin with the pieces of wood on top. While they are doing that, you are off and hiding and then they have got to find you.

Mr Winter

We used to go to the Trocette in the Old Kent Road. They used to have a picture house - you know where the Bingo Hall is, over on the corner there - and there used to be one called the Rialto. That was a posh one. If you was posh you'd go in there. It was all nice inside. Years ago I remember them putting a film on and you used to have to take a bit of brass with you to go in free. It was for the war effort. My dad give me this bit of brass, I don't know what it was. You couldn't go in unless you had this bit of brass. I remember going in there and seeing this film. It was called 'Bluebird'.

May Roberts

If you went to the pictures during the war and the siren went, they always used to put it up on the screen, "The air raid warning is now being sounded. If you want to leave the theatre, do so now." But you could stay in there. If you wanted to take the chance you stayed in there. You got to the point where you thought, "If I go outside I can get killed so I might as well see the film and if I'm going to get killed I'll get killed in here." You were very fatalistic.

Doreen Davis

One thing I used to listen to during the war, if I could talk my mother into letting me listen to it, was called "The Man in Black". Valentine Diall. He used to tell ghostly, eerie stories and if our dad was fire-watching or he was off and it was his night for the wardens I used to plead with my mother to let me stay up late so as I could listen. He used to come on about ten o'clock at night. Around that time I should have been in bed. I think she only let me stay up because she used to be frightened to listen to it on her own. We used to sit there together.

Doreen Davis

A pantomime show by a Southwark Civil Defence concert troupe run by Mr Pater.

One of the pleasures of coming home in the early hours of the morning was the American Forces programme. Wherever we'd been on our rambles, we'd get home - this was before I went into the forces - and the thing that kept us going, all us fellas and girls, we all used to listen to that, and wait up until it signed off, and they used to play that lovely tune at the end, you know, lovely.

Joe Scala

We used to do an awful lot of things, made our own entertainment. We never do them now. My brother and my cousin made up this football game and we used to use a farthing and a sixpence and an old penny. The sixpence was the ball and the other things were the players. We used to use a comb. We used to have matchsticks for the goalposts, stuck in plasticene on the table. You used to push the penny with the comb, and play all down this table. We played that for hours. It's a bit like Subbuteo when you think about it. We should have thought of that and patented it!

Doris Stevenson

ROMANCE

The war hurried things up. You felt as if you might never see them again. Best marry them and make the best of it.

Mary Ellmore

There was a bit of kissing and cuddling in the park, but that was about it. You always used to walk up Rye Lane then. There used to be all the boys up there and we used to go into the Black and White Milk Bar and have an ice cream. If you were wealthy you could have a Knickerbocker Glory.

Doris Stevenson

Hardly any serviceman that was serving away from home thought for one minute that his wife or girlfriend were pure - if he did he was very naive, very naive. On the other side, the man was just as bad. I was just as bad. Can't really blame the women. They didn't know whether they was going to be alive tomorrow - with the bombing - why not enjoy themselves while they could?

Two members of Blue Anchor Library

You'd all know the people down the street who'd been going out with Yanks!

Some of the women had a good time 'cause all the Americans and the Canadians was over here. They was all out for nylon stockings. They done all right.

The Germans used to broadcast about how the Americans were having your girls away and all that.

Group at Blue Anchor Library

Well all the men came home at the end of the war, you see, and all the wives got pregnant! It was the bulge! Do you remember the bulge? All the young ladies that were married, and some that weren't, all got pregnant at the same time! And the bulge is 50 now - do you realise that?

Elizabeth Cole

When I went with a chap during the war, when I used to come home I wouldn't dare go indoors so we'd say goodnight and that just round the corner, because my father - Oh Gawd! If any time I'd say, "I'm going to a dance," he'd say, "You been laying yourself on the line! That boy's out there fighting for you!" I think he must have guessed because I'd come in sometimes a bit late. But I used to make this chap I went with say goodnight round the corner, then I'd walk up my road because my father would sometimes think, "She's a long time," so he'd open the door and look up the road.

Doris Platt

Well I got married during the war. I got engaged in the August, and the war broke out in September, and I got married in '41. You know, my husband went away, and then he came back to me and got married, and then he went. But I suppose, maybe the reason that we got married, to be truthful, was also that I could save money, because we'd got no money between us. His allowance - you know, the wife's allowance - I used to put that away, but lived on my own money.

Doris Platt

There was the baby boom straight afterwards, wasn't there? That was to be expected. The men had been away all that amount of time. What can you expect?

Doris Stevenson

Yes, they used to say that people were getting married for the allowance. Some of the women couldn't give two hoots if their men came back or not, some of them.

Queenie Turner

Having a white wedding, I borrowed Bill's sister's wedding dress, but it only just about fitted me! I was quite tubby, because being the only child my parents used to feed me up. So I had to breathe in and hold this great big bouquet of carnations in front of me all day or it looked as though I was pregnant.

You'd be surprised how the family all got together. I mean, you know - you'd got corned beef - you could get a tin of corned beef - and somebody had got a piece of ham, and somebody could make jelly, or blancmange.

People made presents for you. One of Bill's uncles made us a clock, with a great big horrible case like Big Ben with a tiny face on it. Bill's sister went to Regent Street and bought me a box of mixed china, all different cups and saucers. I bet she was terribly pleased to think she's gone over there and come back with this box. It wasn't that important in those days that you had a matching set, because you were grateful.

Bill and Eileen O'Sullivan

I had a terrible experience. I was going out with Jim who was in the regular army. He was going to Gibraltar for a couple of years. Something went on between us. We were supposed to get engaged and we didn't. He come home and he'd spent all his money or something and we didn't get engaged. He said to me, "You're not sure of yourself, are you?" I said, "I'm sure of myself but I don't think you are." He was in the Kings Fusiliers. They was the first lot to go out into France. He got killed out there before it started properly. I don't know if it was the night he got killed, but I know I woke up in the night and I called out "Jim." Well, I was married then to my husband and his name was Den. He said, "What's the matter?" I remember afterwards calling out "Jim."

Mrs Quinlan

Mrs Quinlan in 1942

I was being harassed every time - "When are you going to marry me?" He sort of chased me. "Oh all right, we'll get married."

Grace Shelford

The Americans are wearing their uniforms and they look very nice and it's all happy and dancing. A lot of them married. But suppose he lived in a New York tenement or something like that. You never knew did you? You didn't take the chance.

Some had babies and the Yanks shot off.

We used to dance with them, have a drink with them and perhaps go out but I never got serious, bit frightened really. Our mums wouldn't let us.

But we used to go dancing. Everybody went dancing then. You had to dance.

There were more women knocking about than men.

And a lot of married women whose husbands were away, they were going with the Yanks, weren't they? I didn't approve of that.

Ethel Dorney and Sabina Brooks

We used to go to dances and the fact that we could jive - the girls were round you, wanted to learn to jive. I went to Sauchiehall Street in Glasgow one night and it was Greens Playhouse and we went in there and we started jiving and the girls came over and they wanted to dance and of course the local boys resented that. So they decided to go outside and wait for us. When we got outside we had about 300 yards to go to get to the YMCA - me and about six other guys, all black. A group of about twelve of them was waiting about a hundred yards from the Playhouse. I know they was tooled up because the girls told us that they'd be after us. You talk about sprinting! When we hit the door, it was every man for himself. Luckily we got away, and we never did that no more. When we go in the dance hall, we don't dance, don't dance with the girls because of that. We knew what was coming. It was like that all the way over. When we went to Nuneaton there were Yanks there. That was worse. They couldn't understand the fraternising, black and white. When they come in the dance, they definitely come in the dance for war - we shouldn't be in the dance. But we got down there in numbers and we fight like hell!

You know a funny thing - I was guarding some Italians in Cranwell, Lincolnshire. Now these Italians were prisoners of war. They wore a green uniform. They were working in the fields with the Land Army girls and we were guarding them. Now, the funny thing is, you couldn't walk out with a WAAF or a Land Army girl because her life would be hell, yet these Italians who were supposed to be prisoners of war, were fraternising openly. I thought this was funny.

There was one German Prisoner of War, Hans, and one day he said to me, "Alec" - I'm standing with the rifle, he's having a drink, sitting down in the field - "Have you ever thought what will happen when this war is over?" So I says, "No. I suppose I'll go home. How about you?" He says - he's a cousin of the Messerschmidt family - "After the war I'll be staying at the Savoy. Where will you be?" That gave me food for thought. Later on, after I came out of the RAF and I became a cab driver, every time I picked up a German and took him to the Savoy I wondered if it was Hans. The man is so right!

Mr Elden

VE AND VJ DAY CELEBRATIONS

A Victory Party in Southwark Park Road. Many of the people have been identified by Iris Peile (nee Framen) the baby in the triangular hat in front of the window of number 28.

Well there was a bombed area in Shadwell Road, and we spent all day, us kids (because we had two days off from school, I'll always remember it, I didn't have to do my maths homework!) and we went everywhere we could, finding wood and stuff, you know, to build a bonfire. And my father actually found some fire-works in the shop that we'd had since before the war. The sparklers and a couple of revolving ones - they worked! And I was allowed to stay up till 11 o'clock. We were singing and there was a pub opposite, so they opened all the doors and the piano was sort of drawn towards the door. And I'll always remember the next night, my mother and I took the bus and walked up to St Paul's. And when we got up there, the lights were all focused on the cross above St Paul's and it was reflected in the sky behind. It was a marvellous sight! And all the lights were on the embankment, and we weren't used to having them like that, you see, like a necklace of pearls, all the way down to St Thomas's Hospital, all the way down the river. And I saw Piccadilly, and it was the brightest lights! God, I'd never seen anything like that!

Elizabeth Cole

The thing I remember most was the night prior to VE Day. We knew it was coming. For weeks where I worked we had been making these little flags that you stuck over and they could be strung across the road. I was listening to the radio. We'd been told, should the war be over, we would have the day off. I was listening to the radio and it suddenly came through that Churchill had said the war was over. That night stuck out more in my mind to think, "Thank God it's finished." Even now I feel so happy. It really was wonderful. The next day we had the parties.

I know me and Frank went out that night and my uncle came in. He'd been out with his friends and I said, "It's over, Frank." He said, "Let's go and see if we can find a party." We didn't have to go far. We went across Sumner Road and we found a party and there we stayed. We celebrated that night till the early hours of the morning. I didn't go to work the next day. I don't remember what I actually did on VE Day. I remember that night. That night will stand out in my mind. It was so glorious that you thought, "No more war!" You've got to think that at ten years old it started, sixteen years old you suddenly realise that it's over and it was wonderful!

Doreen Davis

VE day, that was the day I deserted! I deserted for the day. I was up near Yarmouth, on Air Sea Rescue. There was going to be this big celebration on VE day, and I just came out on the train, down to London, I went to Whitehall and joined in the festivities, and the next day I went back. No-one knew I'd been gone.

Joe Scala

I had cousins who was still out in Burma, they were all still there. The ones in the European war, you knew they were okay, apart from the ones who had died, but you still had them out there in Burma so you didn't really feel the war was actually finished until the VJ - for me anyway.

Doris Stevenson

I was in the Land Army, and a group of us came up by train - to King's Cross, I think it was. Then you had to walk, because there were too many people. You could have walked on people's heads! It was tremendous! Oh, it was marvellous. Everybody was dancing, kissing one another, you know, arm in arm - it was really fantastic! And remember, we had to go back to work the next day! When we got to the station no trains were running, so we had to sit on the station all night, until the milk train came in. I was back on the tractor that morning.

Ivy Maylan

I came back to London with my kids a few weeks before the end of the war. It was a bit strange at first. There was three years between them, everything was all at sixes and sevens; they didn't really go to school, because nothing was organised or done properly.

Kathleen Ash

I didn't know much about politics, but I remember vividly soon after the war - we lived on a main road - Churchill drove past once, I remember everyone booed him. I remember thinking to myself, God, he just got us through a war and now they're booing him! That's something that sticks in my mind.

Win Mitchell

We had entertainment. Singing songs. They got a piano out. Most of the wartime songs... Rule Britannia... Tipperary... Run Rabbit Run... There were games for the children and races.

Louise Sedgewick

A thing that sticks out in my mind from near the war's end that I shall never ever forget was when you saw the first pictures of the camps being opened. Belsen was the one I remember... And I thought, "How can anybody... How can one nation do that to another nation?" I cried my eyes out when I saw it on the news then, because I thought, "Those poor people."

Still this war was going on with Japan so in a way you were still thinking of any relatives or suchlike you had out in the Far East. Most of mine, except for my Uncle Cyril who was out in that area, most of mine were in the European part.

Doreen Davis

The people were so determined not to go back to the conditions that they'd had to put up with pre-war. And they somehow hoped that if the socialists got in, they would be prepared to do far more for them.

Mary Trivett

You see, what is difficult for you to understand is the depth of deprivation that we lived in. You've got to understand this first, before you can understand how deeply we feel. It was grim to say the least of it. The things you read about in Dickens were happening. If we wanted assistance in those days, our parents had to go before a board; they were called the Board of Guardians. And if you had anything in your home that was saleable, you had to sell that before you could get any assistance whatsoever. And you got food tickets, and you got tickets to get children's shoes. You didn't get money. This is the way they treated people. We're talking about the dignity of human beings, and this is why we feel so strongly, and this is why we all voted Labour.

Lil Patrick

When my husband came home, when we went round there they'd got this big flag out the window on a pole. They lived in a big house with a basement and three floors up in this big house they hung the flag out the window on a pole. My brother-in-law painted a big piece of cardboard, stuck paper over it and painted on it, "Welcome Home" for my husband for when he came home. They had all the neighbours in and they were having tea and cakes as a celebration. People made cakes, made jellies, all sorts of things. You all took it and it was all pooled together.

When my Uncle Will came home from El Alamein he was one of the first in our turning to come home so we decorated the streets with "Welcome Home Will!" and we had everything out and the whole turning turned out to welcome him back. And I think then you think, "Ah, he's alright. Yes, he's back. Its finished!" It was utter relief. A feeling of utter relief. That's all I can say.

Doreen Davis

In a way I think a lot of people were more apprehensive when the war finished. You didn't know what was going to happen. I think people were more apprehensive then. You certainly didn't know what peace was going to be. It's silly after six years of war to say you didn't know what peace was going to be, but you really didn't know what the future was going to hold. All you knew was, there wasn't going to be war there.

Doris Stevenson

They did hold street parties for the younger children up to about nine, and then they held another lot for the nine to fourteen lot. The parents, the families were giving up 'points' - we were still on rations, for goods - or they used to have a little pool and people put in what they could afford - money, goods, whatever - to go towards the party which was held about three or four months after the end of war. Made a good sight to see them all sitting down the street. But I hope it never happens again.

Bill Winter

By VJ Day we knew that it was definitely all over, because people who were with the Japanese... I knew someone who was a prisoner of the Japanese - and we saw that he'd come home; I mean he didn't survive very long when he did come home, but at least he came home. You know, that was a friend of mine's brother, but he didn't live very long afterwards, because he was so thin. But I suppose then, with the Japanese, at least the whole thing was finished then. But there was also the bomb and that... I think that was quite a shock. Yes, I think that made us feel a bit different.

Doris Pratt

Adams Gardens, Brunel Road, Rotherhithe in 1935 (above)
and again in 1949 (below) during its reconstruction

AFTERMATH

I must tell you: I got my demob suit, it was brown, that's right. Well I was really fed up with the army because of what I'd seen in the war and at home, and this is true: you know the little toilet on a train - I opened the window, and I threw my cap out of the window, and I threw my trousers and my things out of the window. I came home with my boots. And all I came home with was my demob suit. So my uniform is on the railway lines!

Well, you know, it was how you felt at the moment, because remember that I'd seen some terrible sights, and I'd been with boys that were boys like me, and lost a lot of them.

Bill O'Sullivan

As you walked through London you saw these open spaces, where they'd started to clear them off. There would just be weed growing, covered in rubble and what-have-you. And funny thing was, buddleia began to come out, spurted everywhere. There was flowers on odd corners where the houses had been bombed - and wild cats, ever so many wild cats about. In fact I knew a man who used to feed them at weekends, where the houses had been bombed and the people had moved away.

Flo Spike

There was one chap, he was in the hands of the Japanese - when he came back I've seen people literally go by him and say, "Hello, Albert, how do you feel?" and you could see the tears in their eyes 'cause he looked dreadful. It was horrible. He's never really ever picked up. But he's still alive and still about.

Ivy Richardson

You could walk out of one job into the other. Easy. I'm talking about the building trade. For years and years, you'd go in and out. You could pack it in when you liked. Take a week off if you got a few bob, knowing you'd get in again.

Joe French

It was terrible for the boy when his dad came home. I always had a photo on the sideboard and I used to say to him, "That's Daddy" and I used to say to him, "Say goodnight to Daddy" and things like that. Course, when my husband came home, my boy was absolutely petrified of him. He wouldn't stay in the same room with him. If I went to the loo he would come and wait outside the door for me. He used to keep saying to me, "Mum, when's that man going?"

Louise Sedgewick

In your twenties, you were probably saying, "Oh, I'll do this, I'll make my living in this direction..." But that was out of the question when we were called up. I mean five years is a long time in your formative years. I did resent it really, but it's always offset by the fact that I came out intact.

Bill Gibson

My husband was bitter. He said he missed such a lot of David growing up. He wanted to do everything for David. David wanted to do everything himself. He thought that he didn't ought to do so much for him. David would get up and the shoes, they would all be clean and done. His clothes would be out ready for him. He'd never had it before. He said "Why does he do it?" It's just that his father had missed out on it so he thought he'd start then.

Ivy Richardson

All your plans, and all your bright ideas never came to anything because there was a question of finding somewhere to live, getting a place ready for the men to come home to, and taking the first job you could get to earn a living. There was none of this Social Security standing by to give you hand-outs. You stood on your own feet or you went without! So it wasn't a question of picking and choosing, it was a question of two weeks rest at home when he came home from Singapore. Two weeks was a luxury, because you had a bit of demob money. But then it was find a job and get to work; we had our roof to keep. So you didn't get a choice.

Mary Gibson

When the war was over, the Council said, "You should go back to the colonies." In England I had a vote. But in the colonies I did not have a vote. I didn't have a vote and I fought for the people in Poland to have a vote. I decided not to live in the colonies as I didn't have a vote in the colonies.

There are more Indians and West Indians who won the VC fighting for the nation per thousand than the British people. These people volunteered to fight for freedom for the mother country. Then the mother country said, "No. We should rule you."

Sam King

One woman - she couldn't have been a lot older than me at the time, I suppose she was in her 20s. She got married to this fellow that used to be in Dockhead, and a bomb dropped, and he was killed right near her. She was only young. Years later I come home and I saw this old woman, and someone said to me, "You know who that is don't you?" I said no, they said, "That's Hannah, do you remember Hannah?" So I said, "No, was that the one that was... " And I remember she was pregnant, she was married, and he died. And in later years, when they told me who she was, she was one of those women that run about the pavement, like a bag-woman, run about and swear at you. But she was a beautiful young girl, and a beautiful young fella she was married to. Expecting a baby, she was all happy. But then he died the night the City was bombed.

Joe Scala

After the war, it seemed to go flat. It sounds an awful thing to say, but a lot of people say this - that we were sort of fed on our nerves, tension, excitement. It seemed to go very flat, didn't it, afterwards?

And I think that's when they started to spoil their children. Because the children had to go without so much during the war, and they had to endure all these horrors, now children were bought presents. It built up and built up, until we became a materialistic society, and children were thoroughly spoiled. And they've grown up, and it's gone on, and got much worse.

Grace Smith-Grogue

I suppose I feel more resentful now you know to think what's happened, to think - did it do any good? They're still fighting out in Yugoslavia, the countries are still up in arms at each other. It makes you think, what was it all in aid of? I mean there was 50 million people lost during the war, 50 million in the world. That is a hell of a lot.

Queenie Turner

People after the war got very selfish. Nobody seemed to want to help. Some people got on their feet very quickly. You could tell that they didn't seem to have as much time for one another. Whereas before they were always helping one another and saying, "Have you got this?" or "Do you need this or that?" Most of the people gradually got on their feet and they seemed as if they wanted to forget it more than anything.

Ivy Richardson

As soon as the war finished, I think it changed. You could go out and buy what you wanted. Then the people who had the money, the people who could afford it, bought it, and those that couldn't went without.

I think it was more of a classless society than it is now. During the war the doors were always open to anybody. Soon afterwards they went in, closed their doors and that was it. You never saw people.

Doris Stevenson

The women who had been on war work had had freedom and money for the first time. They were the people who suffered when the men came back and the war work had finished and they were back to housewives. They were the ones who noticed it because they didn't have the money. They were restricted to housework. There were a lot of break-ups in marriages at that time for this reason because the men came back thinking the women were going to be like they were before, suppressed really, before the war. They came back and these women were now independent women who had shouldered responsibility, run houses and worked and they'd done everything themselves. The men thought they were going to come back and take over and it wasn't like that. These women were now independent.

Visitor to Blue Anchor Library

The war broke everything. People around the dock area mainly evacuated. They moved out. They were bombed out. It broke the community. Then they knocked the old houses down and everybody moved away.

Ours was a very long street. We lived at one end, and I would say to half-way down the street, we all had our children together and all the children went to school together, and there was a bond, there really was, and that didn't go after the war.

Some came back, some stayed where they were. Some of the fellas had married girls from other towns, married girls where they had been stationed and never came back.

After the war we had ten years living in that house in Rotherhithe. Then suddenly we read - and you heard through the grapevine really - that this vast building programme was going to go on, and that you would eventually be moved. And I think if they did that now, they wouldn't scrap the houses, they would modernise them, wouldn't they?

I don't think we would ever have moved, any of us, because my sister lived at number 9, my other sister lived at number 15, my mother lived at number 69 at the end of the street, my brother lived at the next turning. We were all near. We wouldn't have gone at all, but the council pulled down the houses.

It was a long street and my mother's house was pulled down first and she moved right up onto Blackheath. The sisters that lived with her moved there. But there was no room for me anywhere near them then. I had to go somewhere different. My brother that lived at the back, his house wasn't pulled down until after ours, so he went to Deptford, he went on the Evelyn estate. The whole lot was completely scattered.

Kathleen Ash

Before VE day had actually happened, I remember going to the County Hall to see a plan for London for after the war. It was the

Abercrombie Plan, and it's well known in the architectural world. I can remember going to see it and feeling that it had all been worthwhile, and it'll be wonderful when it's all built. I came back, sort of full of the joys of spring as it were, thinking all this terrible tragedy we've been through all these years - now we've got a chance to build a proper London, you know. And I remember telling my father - you know, I was full of it - and he said, "Yes girl. I've heard it all before." Now I've got to the age he was then, I can quite understand why he said that to me. What a shambles they've made of it! What a shambles!

Lil Patrick

We did feel resentful about the effect the war had had on our lives. Oh yes. We all did really. It was really six years out of our lives.

Mrs Quinlan